grace
unbounded

DEVOTIONS FOR LENT
2022

AUGSBURG FORTRESS

Minneapolis

GRACE UNBOUNDED
Devotions for Lent 2022

pISBN 978-1-5064-8198-2
eISBN 978-1-5064-8482-2

Writers: Troy M. Troftgruben (March 2–12), Priscilla Paris-Austin (March 13–19), Bekki Lohrmann (March 20–25), Harvard Stephens Jr. (March 26–April 1), Kimberly Knowle-Zeller (April 2–8), Wilbert "Wilk" Miller (April 9–16)

Editor: Laurie J. Hanson
Cover image: Foggy morning in the mountains with flying birds over hills. iStock/Carmian
Cover design: Alisha Lofgren
Interior design and typesetting: Eileen Engebretson
Interior photos: Page 12: "Homeless Jesus" by Timothy Schmalz, Dominican Order Church and Convent Ciudad Colonial, Santo Domingo, Dominican Republic, photo by Mario Roberto Durán Ortiz / CC-BY-SA-4.0 (https://commons.wikimedia.org/wiki /Category:CC-BY-SA-4.0). All other images © iStock. Used by permission.

The paper used in this publication meets the minimum requirements of American National Standard for Information Sciences—Permanence of Paper for Printed Library Materials, ANSI Z329.48-1984.

Manufactured in the USA.

22   21   1   2   3   4   5

Welcome

Grace Unbounded provides daily devotions for each day from Ash Wednesday to the Resurrection of Our Lord/Vigil of Easter (traditionally known as Holy Saturday). Devotions begin with an evocative image and a brief passage from the Gospel of Luke (the gospel focus for 2022, year C in the Revised Common Lectionary). The writers then bring their unique voices and pastoral wisdom to the texts with quotations to ponder, reflections, and prayers.

In Luke's gospel, Jesus reaches out to all kinds of people. He proclaims good news—in particular, to those experiencing poverty, oppression, or captivity. He responds to those who want healing, welcomes time with children, shows great regard for women, shares meals with "unsavory" characters, and seeks out people who have lost their way. No limits, no restrictions, no boundaries—not even death—can stop Christ's love and grace for all people.

May the Spirit empower us each day to love God, and to love one another as God has loved us—with grace unbounded!

Jesus, thou art all compassion,
pure, unbounded love thou art;
visit us with thy salvation,
enter ev'ry trembling heart.
—"Love divine, all loves excelling," ELW 631

Ash Wednesday / March 2

Luke 3:1-3

In the fifteenth year of the reign of Emperor Tiberius, when
Pontius Pilate was governor of Judea, and Herod was ruler of
Galilee, . . . during the high priesthood of Annas and Caiaphas,
the word of God came to John son of Zechariah in the wilderness. He went into all the region around the Jordan, proclaiming a
baptism of repentance for the forgiveness of sins.

To ponder

When our Lord and Master Jesus Christ said, "Repent," he
desired the entirety of believers' lives to be one of repentance. . . .
However, it does not refer solely to an interior repentance. Indeed,
an interior repentance is worth nothing, unless it outwardly pro-
duces various constructive changes.—Martin Luther, *95 Theses*

Changing course

Repentance readies us to welcome Jesus. That's why John proclaimed a "baptism of repentance."

Many of us have baggage with "repentance" language. We associate it with feeling bad—about our choices, our shortcomings, and ourselves. We tend to think *repentance* means getting down on ourselves, in self-centered ways, even though that accomplishes absolutely nothing. Is this really what God wants?

In the New Testament, repentance does not require negative feelings. The word (*metanoia* in Greek) simply means "change of mind/thinking." After all, a change of thinking can change the entire course of our lives.

Repentance is what my phone navigational app helps me do after I take a wrong turn (which happens often): it recalculates a better path. Repentance isn't a pity party. It's what happens when I realize I'm going the wrong way. And if I keep going, someone may get hurt.

To prepare for Jesus, John calls us to repentance. To repent is simply to recalibrate or recalculate our life's course to better embrace Jesus and the reign of God.

Prayer

O God, open my ears to hear Jesus' call, open my eyes to see where I'm heading, and open my hands to be led by your Spirit. Amen.

March 3

Luke 3:21-22

Now when all the people were baptized, and when Jesus also had been baptized and was praying, the heaven was opened, and the Holy Spirit descended upon him in bodily form like a dove. And a voice came from heaven, "You are my Son, the Beloved; with you I am well pleased."

To ponder

Over the years I have come to realize that the greatest trap in our life is not success, popularity, or power, but self-rejection. Success, popularity, and power can, indeed, present a great temptation, but their seductive quality often comes from the way they are part of the much larger temptation to self-rejection. . . . Self-rejection is the greatest enemy of the spiritual life because it contradicts

6

the sacred voice that calls us the "Beloved." Being the Beloved expresses the core truth of our existence.—Henri J. M. Nouwen, *Life of the Beloved*

Beloved

Jesus' baptism is an extraordinary experience: heaven opens, the Spirit descends, and God speaks clearly and directly. Many of us would welcome so direct an encounter with the divine today. Maybe we need not look far.

Only in Luke's gospel is this event associated with prayer. Jesus is praying when something extraordinary happens. We often focus on the extraordinary events, but maybe we should ponder more what precedes them (baptism and prayer). After all, the story suggests that acts of worship and prayer enable us to welcome the Spirit's presence and to hear God speak.

Whether or not we have so extraordinary an encounter, by affirming our baptisms and spending time in prayer we open ourselves to God's words of promise. You are beloved. You have been sealed by the Holy Spirit and marked with the cross of Christ forever. With you, God is profoundly pleased.

We do not need heaven to open in dramatic fashion to hear God speak today: *You are my beloved child.*

Prayer

O God, help us hear your voice speaking to us today, affirming who we are in you. Through Christ our Lord. Amen.

March 4

Luke 4:1-2, 13

Jesus, full of the Holy Spirit, returned from the Jordan and was led by the Spirit in the wilderness, where for forty days he was tempted by the devil. . . . When the devil had finished every test, he departed from him until an opportune time.

To ponder

The first thing that struck me when I came to live in a house with mentally handicapped people was that their liking or disliking me had absolutely nothing to do with any of the many useful things I had done until then. . . . In a way, it seemed as though I was starting my life all over again. . . . This experience was and, in many ways, is still the most important experience of my new life, because it forced me to rediscover my true identity.—Henri J. M. Nouwen, *In the Name of Jesus*

Times of trial

Right after his baptism, Jesus enters the wilderness. In fact, the Spirit leads him there—to be tested. We often regard temptation and testing as bad things to "get through," nothing more. But the Spirit's leading here suggests otherwise.

Unique to Luke's version of this story, the Holy Spirit appears twice at the start and immediately afterward. However lonely Jesus may feel, he is never alone. In fact, the Spirit is nearer at hand here than anywhere else in Luke's narrative.

At some level, this test prepares Jesus for public ministry. It also solidifies the identity God declared at his baptism. At a critical juncture, this experience of testing clarifies who Jesus is. Without it, his ministry would never have been the same.

Times of trial and testing are neither punishments nor signs of God's disfavor. Nor are they pass/fail exams. They help us realize our identity, our purpose, and our support network—even if it feels like we fail. Our trials are seasons for relearning who we are, where we are going, and whose we are.

Prayer

Lord Jesus, in our trials, help us know that you love us, you lead us, and you will never forsake us. Amen.

March 5

Luke 4:14, 16-17

Then Jesus, filled with the power of the Spirit, returned to Galilee. . . . When he came to Nazareth, where he had been brought up, he went to the synagogue on the sabbath day, as was his custom. He stood up to read, and the scroll of the prophet Isaiah was given to him.

To ponder

In a culture that craves the big, the entertaining, the dramatic, and the shocking (sometimes literally), cultivating a life with space for silence and repetition is necessary for sustaining a life of faith.
—Tish Harrison Warren, *Liturgy of the Ordinary*

The sacred in the ordinary

Where does God meet us? Most often it is not in extraordinary and dramatic events, but in the ordinary and routine acts of everyday faith.

After the extraordinary experiences of his baptism and testing, Jesus returns home to Galilee. He visits his hometown, Nazareth. Here and throughout Galilee, "as was his custom," he attends synagogue, gathers with others, worships, and reads and teaches from scripture. There is nothing particularly extraordinary about these acts. Although in Mark's gospel Jesus begins his ministry with calling disciples and miracles, in Luke's gospel Jesus begins with the ordinariness of reading scripture in the synagogue.

This ordinary beginning shows us something. It suggests that the groundwork for ministry and faith is not spiritual mountaintop experiences, but everyday acts of spirituality like worship, reading scripture, silence, prayer, and service. These everyday acts are the bedrock of our connection to God. They are where God most often meets us. They are where the extraordinary happens.

Prayer

Holy Spirit, help us see the significance of our ordinary lives as sacred spaces where you meet us. Give us grace, strength, and courage each day, that we may love God, serve our neighbors, and follow Christ in everyday living. Amen.

Luke 4:17-19

[Jesus] unrolled the scroll and found the place where it was written: "The Spirit of the Lord is upon me, because he has anointed me to bring good news to the poor. He has sent me to proclaim release to the captives and recovery of sight to the blind, to let the oppressed go free, to proclaim the year of the Lord's favor."

To ponder

The gospel of Jesus is not a rational concept to be explained in a theory of salvation, but a story about God's presence in Jesus' solidarity with the oppressed, which led to this death on the cross. What is redemptive is the faith that God snatches victory out of defeat, life out of death, and hope out of despair.—James Cone, *The Cross and the Lynching Tree*

Homeless Jesus

Jesus reads from Isaiah 61:1-2 (compare this with Isaiah 58:6). This text distills Jesus' opening sermon and what his ministry will be about in Luke's gospel. Jesus brings "good news to the poor," release to captives, and freedom to the oppressed. These themes resonate with the year of jubilee, an Israelite practice of debt forgiveness that equalized socioeconomic distinctions (Leviticus 25). Apparently Jesus is focused not simply on interior spirituality. He comes for a socioeconomic reckoning.

Outside St. Alban's Episcopal Church in Davidson, North Carolina, is a sculpture of a man sleeping on a park bench. His feet have wound marks. The sculpture is Timothy Schmalz's "Homeless Jesus." At its installation, reactions varied. Someone called it an "insulting depiction" that "demeaned" the neighborhood. Another called the police, thinking it was a real person. Another said "it creeps him out."

This is the Jesus we find in our reading: a Jesus who identifies with the poor. How does this Jesus speak to you today—to comfort, to challenge, and to call you to bear "good news" to others?

Prayer

O Jesus Christ, speak good news to our poverty; rouse us from complacency; help us bear good news in your name today. Amen.

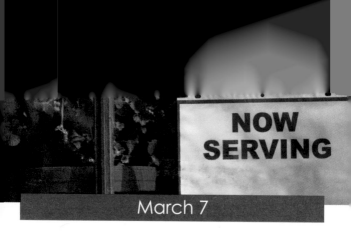

March 7

Luke 4:20-21

And [Jesus] rolled up the scroll, gave it back to the attendant, and sat down. The eyes of all in the synagogue were fixed on him. Then he began to say to them, "Today this scripture has been fulfilled in your hearing."

To ponder

Today your gate is open, and all who enter in / Shall find a Father's welcome and pardon for their sin. / The past shall be forgotten, a present joy be giv'n, A future grace be promised, a glorious crown in heav'n.—"Today your mercy calls us," LBW 304

This is the day

Throughout Luke's gospel, "today" is when Jesus saves.

At Jesus' birth, the angel declares: "To you is born this day [today] . . . a Savior" (2:11). At the synagogue in Nazareth, Jesus claims that "today" Isaiah's prophetic words are "fulfilled in your hearing" (4:21). "Today," Jesus tells Zacchaeus, "salvation has come to this house" (19:9). And to a crucified thief, Jesus promises: "Today you will be with me in Paradise" (23:43). Very distinctively, Luke pegs "today" as the time when Jesus brings salvation.

How does Jesus do this for you today? How is Jesus at work saving, healing, guiding, encouraging, and helping you today? For us too Christ draws near in the present moment to save.

One of my mother's favorite scripture verses was "This is the day that the LORD has made; let us rejoice and be glad in it" (Psalm 118:24). She always carried with her a coin inscribed with that verse, especially during her years of fighting cancer. It reminded her that this day—today—God in Christ is near to save. We can claim this same promise for ourselves today.

Prayer

O Jesus Christ, today remember us. Today save us. Today help us. Today embrace us. Amen.

March 8

Luke 6:6-10

[Jesus] entered the synagogue and taught, and there was a man there whose right hand was withered. The scribes and the Pharisees watched him to see whether he would cure on the sabbath, so that they might find an accusation against him. Even though he knew what they were thinking, he said to the man who had the withered hand, "Come and stand here." He got up and stood there. Then Jesus said to them, "I ask you, is it lawful to do good or to do harm on the sabbath, to save life or to destroy it?" After looking around at all of them, he said to him, "Stretch out your hand." He did so, and his hand was restored.

To ponder

Anytime the Bible is used to justify the oppression and exploitation of others, we have strayed far from the God who brought Israel out of Egypt.—Rachel Held Evans, *Inspired*

The bigger picture

Jesus is on the side of life and doing good. Period.

Stories like this portray the religious leaders, in Jesus' experience, negatively. But they were not scoundrels. They simply valued specific practices of faith highly—too highly. And their focus on specifics kept them from seeing the bigger picture.

We are not much different. We too prefer the predictable over the challenging. We too want a Jesus who fits our expectations. We too want a faith that is manageable, not radical. We too prefer predictable structure over an unpredictable Holy Spirit.

In many ways, Jesus comforted the afflicted and afflicted the comfortable. Our challenge is to embrace this Jesus—including the ways he challenges us, messes up our routines, and calls us to a better life. After all, this Jesus came to bring good, to give life, and to save. Our challenge is simply to welcome him.

Prayer

O Jesus Christ, enter our lives, change our hearts, and reorient us to better things. Give us life and call us again to follow you. Amen.

Luke 6:17, 19-21

[Jesus] stood on a level place, with a great crowd of his disciples and a great multitude of people from all Judea, Jerusalem, and the coast of Tyre and Sidon.... And all in the crowd were trying to touch him, for power came out from him and healed all of them. Then he looked up at his disciples and said:
"Blessed are you who are poor, for yours is the kingdom of God.
"Blessed are you who are hungry now, for you will be filled.
"Blessed are you who weep now, for you will laugh."

To ponder

[A] brash young physicist who had rehearsed all the reasons for atheism [once] arrogantly concluded, "Therefore I do not believe in God." [A] little priest, not put off at all, replied quietly, "Oh, it doesn't matter. God believes in you."—Desmond Tutu, *God Has a Dream*

Blessed and beloved

In biblical times, many believed that God's blessing took shape through material things: riches, health, social honor, work success, and family. Conversely, God's displeasure appeared through poverty, illness, social shame, failure, and dysfunction. Even more, both realities (blessing, disfavor) resulted from something you—or your ancestors—did. Whatever your lot in life, it was earned.

Many today believe the same thing. We deem wealthy celebrities "blessed." We wonder if some who suffer are on God's "bad list."

Jesus thinks that philosophy is baloney. He says so in Luke's beatitudes: "Blessed are you who are poor, . . . who are hungry now, . . . who weep now," because "yours is the kingdom of God." Contrary to all assumptions, Jesus says God is on the side of those the world calls "cursed." God stands with them. God blesses them. God's favor rests on them.

When you feel cursed, Christ is with you. When society snubs you, God blesses you. When people deem you "accursed," the Holy Spirit calls you "beloved."

Prayer

O God, by your Spirit help me to know your blessing, to recognize it in others, and to pass it on to those most needing a blessing in Jesus' name. Amen.

Luke 7:11-13

Soon afterwards [Jesus] went to a town called Nain, and his disciples and a large crowd went with him. As he approached the gate of the town, a man who had died was being carried out. He was his mother's only son, and she was a widow; and with her was a large crowd from the town. When the Lord saw her, he had compassion for her and said to her, "Do not weep."

To ponder

Compassion asks us to go where it hurts, to enter into places of pain, to share brokenness, fear, confusion and anguish. Compassion challenges us to cry out with those in misery, to mourn with those who are lonely, to weep with those in tears. . . . When we look at compassion this way, it becomes clear that something more is involved than a general kindness or tenderheartedness.—Henri J. M. Nouwen, *Compassion*

Compassion

Our experiences of grief and sadness affect Jesus on a visceral level.

In a story preserved only by Luke, Jesus encounters a funeral procession in a little town called Nain. The scene is a sad one: a young man has died. Moreover, he is the only son of a widow. In first-century Judea, widows with no sons had no means of financial support. This woman has lost not only her son but also her livelihood.

At this encounter, Jesus is moved with compassion (*esplanch-nisthē* in Greek). Luke's chosen word indicates a visceral emotion of sympathy. The object of Jesus' compassion, however, is not the young man but the woman. She is the focus of Jesus' emotional response. We find here a Savior deeply affected by our pain. Whether or not Jesus heals, he feels our experience on a visceral level and stops to draw near.

What grief or pain do you now experience? Jesus sees you, knows your pain, and has compassion. Even if he does not change your situation, he stands with you, comforts you, and says:"Do not weep."

Prayer

Lord Jesus, see our burdens, behold our pain, still our weeping, and be near us in suffering. We pray in your name. Amen.

March 11

Luke 7:14-17

[Jesus] came forward and touched the bier, and the bearers stood still. And he said, "Young man, I say to you, rise!" The dead man sat up and began to speak, and Jesus gave him to his mother. Fear seized all of them; and they glorified God, saying, "A great prophet has risen among us!" and "God has looked favorably on his people!" This word about him spread throughout Judea and all the surrounding country.

To ponder

I confess that I too used to be embarrassed by talk about heaven and an afterlife. It seemed a cop-out, a crutch. . . . But I've changed over the years, mainly as I've watched people die. What kind of

God would be satisfied forever with a world like this one, laden with suffering and death?—Philip Yancey, *Where Is God When It Hurts?*

The last word

Although this story resonates with other prophetic miracles in scripture (1 Kings 17:17-24; 2 Kings 4:18-37), in Luke's gospel this is the first time Jesus raises the dead. Risking ritual defilement, Jesus stops the funeral procession by touching the bier. More remarkably, he speaks just four, brief words (in Greek)— and in doing so raises life out of death.

This story is not a random incident. It shows us a Jesus who will not stand idly by at a funeral. It shows us a God who will not let death have the last word.

What if Jesus did something similar at the next funeral you attend, . . . the next loss in your life, . . . the next community tragedy? Jesus came not simply to teach and welcome. He came to raise the dead. He comes to do the same for you—in and beyond this earthly life.

In Lent, we travel to the cross with One who will make sure that death does not have the final word.

Prayer

God who raised our Lord Jesus, by your Spirit raise new life in us and around us today, tomorrow, and forevermore. Amen.

March 12

Luke 7:18-20, 22

John summoned two of his disciples and sent them to the Lord. . . . When the men had come to him, they said, "John the Baptist has sent us to you to ask, 'Are you the one who is to come, or are we to wait for another?'" . . . And he answered them, "Go and tell John what you have seen and heard: the blind receive their sight, the lame walk, the lepers are cleansed, the deaf hear, the dead are raised, the poor have good news brought to them."

To ponder

We may wish for answers, but God rarely gives us answers. Instead, God gathers us up into soft, familiar arms and says, "Let me tell you a story."—Rachel Held Evans, *Inspired*

Welcome the journey

We often want clear answers from God to our questions. But God in Christ is less interested in answers than in journeys of discernment.

In our text, John asks Jesus a question. It's a straightforward one. It invites one of two answers. Jesus could have responded with a word—and John would have been happy.

But Jesus doesn't do that. Instead, he recounts recent events, inviting John to consider: "Here is what's happened. What do you think?"

I've experienced similar responses to my questions. I routinely ask God for answers—often by yes/no questions. I rarely get easy answers. Most often, I am prompted to consider scripture, recent events, and others' input. Instead of answers, I sense an invitation to engage God in prayer and the Holy Spirit in discernment.

In the gospels, Jesus loves questions far more than answers. After all, questions begin conversation; answers end it. Questions start new journeys; answers often stop them.

If Jesus doesn't answer your questions quickly, don't be offended. He'd rather start a journey with you than end it.

Prayer

O Jesus Christ, lead us in discernment as we strive to journey faithfully, to hear your voice, and to embrace your presence. Amen.

March 13 / Lent 2

Luke 8:1-3

[Jesus] went on through cities and villages, proclaiming and bringing the good news of the kingdom of God. The twelve were with him, as well as some women who had been cured of evil spirits and infirmities: Mary, called Magdalene, from whom seven demons had gone out, and Joanna, the wife of Herod's steward Chuza, and Susanna, and many others, who provided for them out of their resources.

To ponder

And let us consider how to provoke one another to love and good deeds, not neglecting to meet together, as is the habit of some, but encouraging one another, and all the more as you see the Day approaching.—Hebrews 10:24-25

Travel companions

When planning a trip, I am always attentive to who my travel companions will be. I am likely to seek out hotels with Wi-Fi™, pools, and generous breakfast buffets for a family trip, whereas for a trip with my friends I might look for a more rustic, isolated setting. Who I travel with also affects what I bring and what I do during the journey. When traveling with work colleagues, I'll bring along books to share. With my sister, I might bring a sewing kit and walking shoes. With my children, I am sure to bring board games and snacks—lots of snacks!

Jesus chooses a diverse group of travel companions: people of varied genders, social statuses, needs, gifts, and resources. This is a model of inclusivity, as well as of care and humility. Jesus is teacher and guide, as well as the recipient of companionship and care. Jesus' companions both shape and allow for his ministry to be what it will be.

With whom are you traveling on your baptismal journey? How are you being shaped by your companions? How are you traveling like Jesus, offering and receiving care?

Prayer

God with us, open our hearts to welcome a variety of companions on our spiritual journeys. Make us generous in our giving, so that we bring your healing. Make us humble in our receiving, so that we may know your loving care. Amen.

Luke 9:12-13, 16-17

The day was drawing to a close, and the twelve came to [Jesus] and said, "Send the crowd away, so that they may go into the surrounding villages and countryside, to lodge and get provisions; for we are here in a deserted place." But he said to them, "You give them something to eat." They said, "We have no more than five loaves and two fish." . . . And taking the five loaves and the two fish, he looked up to heaven, and blessed and broke them, and gave them to the disciples to set before the crowd. And all ate and were filled.

To ponder

Tomorrow belongs to those who can conceive of it as belonging to everyone, who lend the best of ourselves to it, and with joy.
—Audre Lorde, *A Burst of Light*

Filled

A day filled with teaching, healing, and crowd control was ending. The disciples and Jesus must have been exhausted, but now the people, having been fed spiritually, were bound to need physical nourishment as well. The disciples thought it wise to send the people away for the night; five loaves and two fish would never be enough for everyone.

I wonder how often we, like the disciples, put limits on what God can do for us, with us, and through us. How often are we tempted to settle for "good enough" in our healing, in our relationships, or in that which nourishes us? How often do we hide what we have or what we are from the world, for fear it won't be enough?

In the face of communal need, Jesus wasn't done for the day. He blessed the food that was offered and it became more than enough to feed a whole crowd. And amid all that is happening in our world today, Jesus still isn't done blessing and nourishing people.

Prayer

Nourishing Savior, open our hearts to expect your abundant love and blessing in this world. Teach us to share what we have and what we are, trusting that in you there is always more than enough. Amen.

March 15

Luke 9:28-30, 33-35

Jesus took with him Peter and John and James, and went up on the mountain to pray. And while he was praying, the appearance of his face changed, and his clothes became dazzling white. Suddenly they saw two men, Moses and Elijah, talking to him.... Peter said to Jesus, "Master, it is good for us to be here; let us make three dwellings, one for you, one for Moses, and one for Elijah"—not knowing what he said. While he was saying this, a cloud came and overshadowed them; and they were terrified.... Then from the cloud came a voice that said, "This is my Son, my Chosen; listen to him!"

To ponder

I have begun to realize that the promise of God is presence, not perfection. The promise of God is to conquer death, not to eliminate it. It's not to completely take away the struggle and suffering, but to redeem it.... God is present whether we pray for God's presence or not.—David Scherer, *AGAP-OLOGY*

With Jesus

I've often longed for a mountaintop experience with Jesus: a moment when I am pulled aside, maybe with a couple of other special people, to see clearly the divinity of Christ and hear the booming voice of God. I long to feel that privilege, to see Jesus so clearly, to hear God without having to wonder if it is God. Yet it occurs to me that, even if I had this experience, I might be just like Peter and totally miss the point.

Every day has mountaintop experiences that I, like Peter, keep misinterpreting: the dazzling light of the morning sun as it streams into my bedroom window, the laughter or grumbles of my children as they prepare for the day, the head nod from my neighbor as we both collect our mail.

Jesus is always with us. I repeat: God is all around us. The challenge is, are we listening?

Prayer

God of the mountaintop, I thank you for your abiding presence. Tune my ears to the frequency of your love, that I may hear your voice and follow your Son. Amen.

Luke 10:25-28

A lawyer stood up to test Jesus. "Teacher," he said, "what must I do to inherit eternal life?" He said to him, "What is written in the law? What do you read there?" He answered, "You shall love the Lord your God with all your heart, and with all your soul, and with all your strength, and with all your mind; and your neighbor as yourself." And he said to him, "You have given the right answer; do this, and you will live."

To ponder

I believe that love is the answer to EVERYTHING. I am a lover, first and foremost. A lover of God. A lover of self. A lover of people. A lover of justice. A lover of liberation. A lover of restoration.

A lover of healing. A lover of wholeness.—Rozella Haydée White (@lovebigcoach), June 3, 2020

Love

The message of all the scriptures comes down to one thing: love God, love self, love neighbor. It's a simple message and yet we manage to screw it up, time and time again. We forget that love is more than a feeling, and we fail to live love as an active verb. We are so rigid in our understanding of what loving God looks like that we lose sight of the liberation it is meant to reveal; we place so much focus on law and obedience that we forget God's grace and mercy. We take love of self to extremes by thinking only of ourselves or by believing that we are unworthy of love and care. We imagine God in our own image rather than seeing God's image in us and all our neighbors in the world. We allow petty arguments to fracture relationships.

Love is a daily practice of engaging our heart, mind, body, and spirit in caring for God, ourselves, our families, our friends, our enemies, and our neighbors—those we know and those we have yet to know.

Prayer

Divine Love, teach us your way of being. Inspire us to live like Jesus, the embodiment of love. Help us to love so we may live. Amen.

Luke 10:29-32

But wanting to justify himself, [the man] asked Jesus, "And who is my neighbor?" Jesus replied, "A man was going down from Jerusalem to Jericho, and fell into the hands of robbers, who stripped him, beat him, and went away, leaving him half dead. Now by chance a priest was going down that road; and when he saw him, he passed by on the other side. So likewise a Levite, when he came to the place and saw him, passed by on the other side."

To ponder

Philanthropy is commendable but it must not cause the philanthropist to overlook the circumstances of economic injustice which make philanthropy necessary.—Martin Luther King Jr., *Strength to Love*

Passing by

As I walk in my neighborhood, I encounter a wide variety of people: children on scooters, an elder receiving assistance with their walker, men chatting while they smoke, people out walking their dogs, a woman pushing an overflowing shopping cart, spry elders out for a jog, busy shoppers heading to the mall, hobby enthusiasts operating motorized toy boats in the park fountain, and folks sitting by watching. All these people are my neighbors, but more often than I wish to admit, when I see them, I am just passing by. This isn't out of derision or scorn, or even out of any intentional desire to ignore them, yet it's what I do. I pass by, often on the other side of the street.

I have deep empathy for the priest and the Levite who are convicted in Jesus' parable, because they are me. I'm busy. I trust that someone else will come along. I believe it's none of my business. I'm scared to get involved. And every time this happens, I am passing by my neighbor. Did you see her? Or are you passing by too?

Prayer

Dear Jesus, open my eyes and my heart to see my neighbors, especially those in need. Help me to pause and take time to be a neighbor to all. Amen.

March 18

Luke 10:33-37

[Jesus continued,] "But a Samaritan . . . was moved with pity. He went to him and bandaged his wounds. . . . Then he put him on his own animal, brought him to an inn, and took care of him. The next day he took out two denarii, gave them to the innkeeper, and said, 'Take care of him; and when I come back, I will repay you whatever more you spend.' Which of these three, do you think, was a neighbor to the man who fell into the hands of the robbers?" He said, "The one who showed him mercy." Jesus said to him, "Go and do likewise."

To ponder

God's word is like water. As God's word works through our lives, our communities, and our nations, it enables growth, rejuvenates communities, and then is recycled again. Even with God's word, we do not own it but must recirculate it, again and again offering blessings to all who receive it.—Eric H. F. Law, *Holy Currencies*

Do likewise

Open to an interruption of his plans, the Samaritan shares his time, his resources, his healing skills, and his network of people to care for the stranger he found beaten on the side of the road. In a world where hoarding of resources and scarcity thinking abound, this behavior is bizarre and confusing. What if the Samaritan were to need those resources later? Did he really have time or energy to return and check on this fellow later? The Samaritan is an extraordinary person indeed.

Or perhaps the Samaritan is simply not bound by such limited thinking. Perhaps he knows that everything he has is a gift from God to be shared. Perhaps he experienced similar generosity of care from someone in the past. And, if so, what generosity is now inspired in the innkeeper and in the stranger, once he recovers from his injuries?

Prayer

Generous Love, you show up in our lives before we ask and shower us with your blessings. Keep us humble so that we can be like the Samaritan and share your blessings with others, trusting that your abundance will always return to us, again and again. Amen.

March 19

Luke 11:1-4

[Jesus] was praying in a certain place, and after he had finished, one of his disciples said to him, "Lord, teach us to pray." . . . He said to them, "When you pray, say:
Father, hallowed be your name.
Your kingdom come.
Give us each day our daily bread.
And forgive us our sins,
for we ourselves forgive everyone indebted to us.
And do not bring us to the time of trial."

To ponder

I lift up my eyes to the hills—
from where will my help come?
My help comes from the LORD,
who made heaven and earth.
—Psalm 121:1-2

Forgive us

A posture of humility is at the center of this prayer that Jesus teaches us. *God* is holy. *God* has a vision for this world. *God* provides for our needs. *God* is the starting point for resolving our conflicts. *God* is our protector. By learning this prayer, we are reminded of our brokenness and our need for God.

Many of the conflicts and tragedies around us—violence, oppression, war, famine, climate change, and more—are rooted in our human selfishness and "me first" mentality. This prayer is more than a conversation with God; it is a guide for shifting our focus from ourselves to the one who is holy, the one who wants the best for all of us and this world.

Let us pray the way Jesus taught us.

Prayer

Divine Love, show us your vision and give us what we need— nothing more and nothing less. Keep our focus on you. Thank you for your saving love. Amen.

March 20 / Lent 3

Luke 11:5, 8-9

[Jesus] said to them, "Suppose one of you has a friend, and you go to him at midnight and say to him, 'Friend, lend me three loaves of bread.' . . . I tell you, even though he will not get up and give him anything because he is his friend, at least because of his persistence he will get up and give him whatever he needs. So I say to you, Ask, and it will be given you; search, and you will find; knock, and the door will be opened for you."

To ponder

I have a real tricky time hearing folks that don't believe in themselves.—*Ted Lasso*

Fully gestated prayers

Jesus tells a story about a guy who seriously believes in himself and is banging down his neighbor's door in the middle of the night. His prayer is fully formed. What if that's God's desire for us, for our own sake, that we would have fully gestated prayers dwelling in us, dictating our actions? People who have fully gestated prayers are a force to be reckoned with. Think of Martin Luther King Jr. Think of the protesters on the street in the summer of 2020.

In the Apple TV+ series *Ted Lasso*, the lowly water boy has a great idea to share with the coach, which he shares timidly, mumbling as if his idea warrants little attention. The coach shares today's "To ponder" quote. The most important thing to the coach is that the water boy develop his voice, his conviction.

What if that is God's desire for us? What if it is this power that God is cultivating in us for the sake of the world?

Prayer

Patient God, grow your fully formed desires for this world in our hearts that, aware of these desires, we might persist until they have come to fruition, for Jesus' sake. Amen.

March 21

Luke 13:10-13

Now [Jesus] was teaching in one of the synagogues on the sabbath. And just then there appeared a woman with a spirit that had crippled her for eighteen years. She was bent over and was quite unable to stand up straight. When Jesus saw her, he called her over and said, "Woman, you are set free from your ailment." When he laid his hands on her, immediately she stood up straight and began praising God.

To ponder

As Black mothers, grief is embedded in our being. It accumulates and manifests as body aches and pains. But many of us have never been taught how to deal with it.—A. Rochaun Meadows-Fernandez, "The Unbearable Grief of Black Mothers"

It must be otherwise

There are indeed a great many spirits that burden many women in our world: mothers who fear for their sons' lives due to the color of their skin; women with no children who have internalized that they are somehow less than their mothering peers; women who make themselves small to avoid attracting unwanted, threatening attention—to name just a few.

Possibly the most debilitating of spirits is the spirit in our culture that sees a woman suffering, bent low by all that society has laid on her, and asks, "What could *you* do differently so as to not be so bent and broken? How could you have dressed differently, how could you have spoken differently, how could you have raised your children differently?"

It is a glorious triumph for women and downtrodden people everywhere that Jesus does not ask the woman any of this. Jesus simply recognizes that she is bent low and insists that it must be otherwise, and he raises her upright.

Prayer

God, before we ask this world's downtrodden souls to change themselves from within, teach us what it is that must be changed from without, and give us the necessary courage to get to work unburdening one another. Amen.

March 22

Luke 14:12-14

[Jesus said,] "When you give a luncheon or a dinner, do not invite your friends or your brothers or your relatives or rich neighbors, in case they may invite you in return, and you would be repaid. But when you give a banquet, invite the poor, the crippled, the lame, and the blind. And you will be blessed, because they cannot repay you, for you will be repaid at the resurrection of the righteous."

To ponder

"I invited homies from the crew—you know *vatos* like me who didn't had no place to go for Christmas."

He names the five homies who came over—all former enemies from rival gangs.

44

" . . . you're not gonna believe this . . . but . . . I cooked a turkey."
You can feel his pride right through the phone.

" . . . Yeah. The six of us, we just sat there, staring at the oven,
waiting for the turkey to be done."—Greg Boyle, *Tattoos on the
Heart*

What an honor

How we respond to Jesus' call to host a meal for those who cannot
pay us back says something about our position in society. Some of
us will get to work—it might feel like a chore now, but we'll reap
dividends in heaven, so, okay, we'll put together the invite list. To
others, if feels like the honor of a lifetime to even be considered as
the host for a meal.

Miguel, the host of a humble Christmas dinner in *Tattoos on
the Heart*, had suffered through a traumatic childhood. Hosting
his first Christmas dinner, for five guys from rival gangs—none of
whom were going to advance his personal agenda—made him feel
like royalty.

What if this call of Jesus isn't about doing what is right as part
of a heavenly rewards program, but is about letting Jesus reveal to
us that we really have something to offer—something that really
matters?

Prayer

Inviting God, thank you for regarding us as worthy to serve your
most treasured, beloved people. It's an honor to be considered for
this. Amen.

March 23

Luke 15:1-2

Now all the tax collectors and sinners were coming near to listen to [Jesus]. And the Pharisees and the scribes were grumbling and saying, "This fellow welcomes sinners and eats with them."

To ponder

A truly Christian work is it that we descend and get so mixed up in the mire of the sinner as deeply as he sticks there himself, taking his sin upon ourselves and floundering out of it with him, not acting otherwise than as if his sin were our own.—Martin Luther, "Third Sunday after Trinity: Luke 15:1-10"

Sinking in

Imagine sinking your teeth into your favorite food, every part of you giving in to the joyful experience of the flavors and textures. Imagine sinking your whole body into your favorite armchair, the way it feels to let every part of yourself ease into the cushions.

So much of Christianity over the centuries has focused us on rising above, escaping, or purifying ourselves from this world. We've internalized the notion that this world is a source of contamination that we must keep away from in order to preserve ourselves for God.

Jesus, however, treats the world like an armchair, sinking all the way into it. Jesus sinks his teeth into his food, eaten beside sinners, finding joy in the experience of its flavors and textures. He spends no energy trying to preserve or purify himself by hovering above this world.

What is God calling you to sink more deeply into today?

Prayer

Creator, it is a wonder that you have found this world worth sinking into, giving yourself to us fully. Guide me that I too might sink down into this earth, feet firmly planted, mixed up thoroughly in the trickiness that is humanity. Amen.

March 24

Luke 15:3-6

[Jesus] told them this parable: "Which one of you, having a hundred sheep and losing one of them, does not leave the ninety-nine in the wilderness and go after the one that is lost until he finds it? When he has found it, he lays it on his shoulders and rejoices. And when he comes home, he calls together his friends and neighbors, saying to them, 'Rejoice with me, for I have found my sheep that was lost.'"

To ponder

We are misled by the religious pictures which depict Jesus . . . carrying a cuddly white lamb on his shoulder. A lamb will hardly stray from its mother. It is the troublesome, obstreperous sheep which is likely to go astray, going through the fence, having its

48

wool torn and probably ending up in a ditch of dirty water. It is this dirty, smelly, riotous creature [God] goes after.—Desmond Tutu, *Hope and Suffering*

Feeling found

Today we're not going to worry about identifying "lost sheep" to go after. We're not going to worry about how we are supposed to treat the gnarly, lost sheep in our lives. We're often too quick to try to create an ethic or a to-do list out of God's word of mercy.

Today we're going to pause and notice the times when we were lost—really lost. Let's call to mind the times when we were cold and miserable in a ditch of dirty water, tattered and riotous. When were we truly undesirable?

Now notice who received us when we were in that state. How did compassion find us and embrace us? Who rejoiced over us and what form did that rejoicing take?

Before we go charging off to find the "lost sheep" of this world, let's remember what God's mercy and grace felt like when we were the lost sheep ourselves. Let's spend some time right now letting our bodies remember what it felt like to be found, cherished, and celebrated, despite our tattered wool.

Prayer

Shepherding Maker, thank you for celebrating me when I was a lost, royal mess. Knowing that part of my own story helps me to see others as you see them when they are in that same state. Amen.

March 25

Luke 15:8-10

[Jesus also said,] "Or what woman having ten silver coins, if she loses one of them, does not light a lamp, sweep the house, and search carefully until she finds it? When she has found it, she calls together her friends and neighbors, saying, 'Rejoice with me, for I have found the coin that I had lost.' Just so, I tell you, there is joy in the presence of the angels of God over one sinner who repents."

To ponder

Repentance (*metanoia* in Greek) means, in essence, to snap out of it. To repent is to think new thoughts, and what makes the Gospel so meaningful is that it offers us a form of brain spackle to fill in the deeply worn neural grooves in our brains, where harmful thoughts have funneled through over and over.—Nadia Bolz-Weber, *Shameless*

Restored to our original shine

So often the stories that Christendom has told about repentance are stories about folks living outside of the church's teachings who begin to conform to the church's teachings.

What if a truly repentant life does not look like conformity to a pre-prescribed vision of rightness, but like snapping out of a limited worldview—the thinking of new thoughts, the envisioning of new visions, the living of a new and formerly unimagined story? What if it is less about someone who is wrong becoming right, and more like an old coin that had been stuck under the rug, now rolled out and restored to its original shine? A sober drunk asking his boss for a promotion, no longer chained to the idea of himself as a failure? A depressed woman buying herself cut flowers, as an act of defiance against the voice that tells her she's not worthy?

God doesn't celebrate our conformity to a one-dimensional understanding of goodness, but celebrates a life once hidden under the rug, now returned to its glimmering shine.

Prayer

Divine Sweeper, snap us out of our old ways and shine us up with the breath of your Spirit, that our glimmer might illumine the way for others who have lost their luster. Amen.

March 26

Luke 15:11-13

Then Jesus said, "There was a man who had two sons. The younger of them said to his father, 'Father, give me the share of the property that will belong to me.' So he divided his property between them. A few days later the younger son gathered all he had and traveled to a distant country, and there he squandered his property in dissolute living."

To ponder

Today we live in a culture of brokenness and fragmentation. Images of individualism and autonomy are far more compelling to us than visons of unity, and the fabric of relatedness seems dangerously threadbare and frayed. . . . The Christian is convinced of a unity which lies deeper, in our very creation and condition, a

oneness which roots in the fact that—despite our strangeness to one another—we are all children of the same creator God.
—Parker J. Palmer, *The Company of Strangers*

A family story

This is one of the most well-known parables in the Bible, and the brilliant narrative operates at many levels. Jesus looks at one family while casting an eye upon all of humanity. When and how were the seeds of such division and estrangement first sown that caused a son to demand of his father, "I want right now what will belong to me"? As the younger sibling quickly squanders his precious inheritance, we are faced with the question: Where am I in a story like this?

Many cross-cultural interpretations of this parable point out how different this story would be if the family and community structures were more intact. Perhaps this is part of Jesus' timeless message to those who walk in his name: What can overcome our separation from God and one another? Why is forgiveness so critical to finding the path toward greater unity with God and others?

Prayer

Holy Father, loving Mother, enfold us with the power of your grace unbounded. At every age, in all circumstances, show us how to live as your children and as a family unified by the wonders of your love. Amen.

Luke 15:14-15, 17-19

"When [the younger son] had spent everything, a severe famine took place throughout that country, and he began to be in need. So he went and hired himself out to one of the citizens of that country, who sent him to his fields to feed the pigs. . . . But when he came to himself he said, 'How many of my father's hired hands have bread enough and to spare, but here I am dying of hunger! I will get up and go to my father, and I will say to him, "Father, I have sinned against heaven and before you; I am no longer worthy to be called your son."'"

To ponder

There is something about the snow-laden sky in winter in the late afternoon / that brings to the heart elation and the lovely meaninglessness of time. / Whenever I get home—whenever—somebody loves me there.—Mary Oliver, "Walking Home from Oak-Head"

Longing for home

No matter the circumstances, there is something universal about our longing to come home—and our expectation that someway, somehow, something good may come of it. When we are desperate to return to the places where we are known, we are often completely willing to swallow our pride to accommodate the swirl of emotions and whatever degree of reconciliation is needed to make peace and find our place again.

Jesus tells this story with great passion. Not only a tale of earthbound yearnings, it also anticipates the hope of the faithful who long for that place we call heaven. Sometimes even a return to church after a long absence bears this hope that whenever I get there again, somebody will love me.

Prayer

Christ our home, our souls are indeed restless until they find their home in your love. Grant us this gift each day. Amen.

Luke 15:20-24

"So [the younger son] set off and went to his father. But while he was still far off, his father saw him and was filled with compassion; he ran and put his arms around him and kissed him. Then the son said to him, 'Father, I have sinned against heaven and before you; I am no longer worthy to be called your son.' But the father said to his slaves, 'Quickly, bring out a robe—the best one—and put it on him; put a ring on his finger and sandals on his feet. And get the fatted calf and kill it, and let us eat and celebrate; for this son of mine was dead and is alive again; he was lost and is found!' And they began to celebrate."

To ponder

Our capacity to forgive always allows us to be in touch with our own agency. . . . Without agency we collapse into passivity, inertia, depression, and despair.—bell hooks, *Sisters of the Yam*

The capacity to forgive

These are the actions of a rich man: people are given orders; fine clothes are presented, along with a beautiful ring; a feast is prepared.

What about the rest of us? What does this story inspire us to do when we celebrate the return of someone we love? Consider the joyful emotions displayed by family and friends of innocent people who win their battle to be released from prison. Remember the spontaneous revelry around COVID-19 hospital patients who recovered and went home.

How remarkable it is when those who have been unfairly made to suffer choose to publicly renounce their feelings of anger and bitterness. Their poignant expressions of forgiveness are remarkable signs of grace unbounded at work.

Prayer

God of grace, forgive us our sins as we forgive those who sin against us. Set us free to live new lives as you fill our stories with the light of your love. Amen.

March 29

Luke 15:25-28

"Now his elder son was in the field; and when he came and approached the house, he heard music and dancing. He called one of the slaves and asked what was going on. He replied, 'Your brother has come, and your father has killed the fatted calf, because he has got him back safe and sound.' Then he became angry and refused to go in."

To ponder

Some fathers give a wound merely by their silence; they are present, yet absent to their sons. . . . My father was gone, but . . . physically still around. . . . So I lived with a wound no one could see or understand. In the case of silent, passive, or absent fathers,

58

the question goes unanswered. "Do I have what it takes? Am I a man, Daddy?"—John Eldredge, *Wild at Heart*

To heal or to do harm

When one son leaves home with an inflated sense of entitlement, his older brother remains behind, perhaps showing loyalty and devotion to his parents. But unanswered questions emerge when the younger son finally returns home. Had anyone recognized the spiritual and emotional needs of the brother who stayed home? Why didn't the older sibling have a stronger sense of belonging and greater confidence that his life mattered, even as his brother was welcomed home?

God knows that our identities are complex and that we are often unprepared for the questions that emerge when our capacities to heal or to do harm to one another are revealed. The mysteries of limitless grace set us free to recognize what our attitudes and behaviors toward others can do. We all have the power to break down or build up essential relationships in the places we call home.

Prayer

Holy God, show us how to grow in your image, for you are gracious and merciful, slow to anger, and abounding in steadfast love. Amen.

March 30

Luke 15:28-29, 31-32

"His father came out and began to plead with him. But he answered his father, 'Listen! For all these years I have been working like a slave for you, and I have never disobeyed your command; yet you have never given me even a young goat.' . . . Then the father said to him, 'Son, you are always with me, and all that is mine is yours. But we had to celebrate and rejoice, because this brother of yours was dead and has come to life; he was lost and has been found.'"

To ponder

Forgiveness allows you to shed your toxic feelings and free yourself of resentments so that the original hurt does not continue to oppress you each day. . . . It is something that happens once we have struggled with our own feelings, searched for meaning, and healed. The process may happen overnight or take years.—Mark I. Rosen, *Thank You for Being Such a Pain*

Now is the time

"We had to celebrate and rejoice," the father insists, having grown wise through his ordeal of rejection and shame. He has found a way to restore his own soul and not remain mired in the difficult experience of seeing his youngest son act so selfishly. Realizing that his eldest son is not ready to bring a spirit of reconciliation to the celebration, now the father must take his stand. If not today, then perhaps one day his eldest son will let go of bitterness and help restore wholeness to the family.

This is what God does through the unbounded grace we are given in the name of Jesus. We follow the One who calls us to tables and fonts and acts of healing, where our doubts and bitterness can give way to the wonders of this invitation: Now is the time for us to celebrate and rejoice.

Prayer

The sounds of amazing grace are always sweet and renewing, and we thank you, almighty God, for inviting us to partake of these gifts. Teach us to share them in our broken world so that your transforming justice will appear in our hearts, our homes, and our communities. Amen.

March 31

Luke 17:12-16, 19

As [Jesus] entered a village, ten lepers approached him. Keeping their distance, they called out, saying, "Jesus, Master, have mercy on us!" When he saw them, he said to them, "Go and show yourselves to the priests." And as they went, they were made clean. Then one of them, when he saw that he was healed, turned back, praising God with a loud voice. He prostrated himself at Jesus' feet and thanked him. And he was a Samaritan.... Then [Jesus] said to him, "Get up and go on your way; your faith has made you well."

To ponder

Wherever it came from, the stroke—and the crisis of faith that it precipitated—was a deep teaching. Faith seems fragile and

intangible when it disappears. Yet it has been the most powerful wellspring in my life and a source of strength since it returned.
—Ram Dass, "Stroked"

Faith rekindled

Faith often surprises us. When we think we have mastered this gift, it may slip away, holding captive our confidence in its power. However, in marvelous and astounding ways, it can also suddenly reappear, connecting us to the signs and wonders of a God who can make all things new.

The story of the ten people affected by leprosy is often shared on days of thanksgiving. The act of returning to the Lord and expressing gratitude for being cleansed from the scourge of this illness is a model we are all called to emulate. Jesus acknowledges this by sending the Samaritan on his way with the clear affirmation "Your faith has made you well."

Many kinds of illness come our way. Some are mental or physical illnesses, while others are social and cultural signs that we have become indifferent to the needs of others. Amid these things, the gifts of unending grace must work first to rekindle the faith that has been lost. And with faith restored, all manner of healing will appear.

Prayer

Now thank we all our God with hearts and hands and voices, for who you are and how your blessings fill our world. Amen.

April 1

Luke 18:15-17

People were bringing even infants to [Jesus] that he might touch them; and when the disciples saw it, they sternly ordered them not to do it. But Jesus called for them and said, "Let the little children come to me, and do not stop them; for it is to such as these that the kingdom of God belongs. Truly I tell you, whoever does not receive the kingdom of God as a little child will never enter it."

To ponder

A healing ministry cannot function without the support of a dedicated prayer group.... Part of every prayer group meeting should be devoted to mentioning the names of persons who have requested prayer.... There should be absolutely no gossip about requests for prayer . . . each member must pray that the power of the Holy Spirit will guide and direct the entire group—and then actually allow [the Spirit] to do so.—Mary Peterman, *Healing*

Let the little children come to me

Here is an example of how children can be trapped in the insecurities of marginal lives. Why would the disciples try to keep people from bringing infants to Jesus? Sometimes scripture shows these barriers overcome by the status of children's parents and guardians, but we are mistaken if we suggest that healing ministry need not include the needs of children and families today.

This is a good time to take inventory of how children are regarded in our faith communities. Who knows their names? Who advocates for their inclusion in worship and church programs? Who looks for them when they are absent, and who offers them support outside of our church buildings? How are their special days celebrated? All of this reflects a critical aspect of ministry to children: the power of the Holy Spirit works in us all, old and young, to reveal the wonders of God's reign.

Prayer

Thank you, Jesus, for all the ways you care for the children we are called to love and serve. Let our prayers for the little ones among us reflect our commitment to help children come to know you. Amen.

April 2

Luke 18:35-43

As [Jesus] approached Jericho, a blind man was sitting by the roadside begging. When he heard a crowd going by, he asked what was happening. They told him, "Jesus of Nazareth is passing by." Then he shouted, "Jesus, Son of David, have mercy on me!" Those who were in front sternly ordered him to be quiet; but he shouted even more loudly, "Son of David, have mercy on me!" Jesus stood still and ordered the man to be brought to him; and . . . he asked him, "What do you want me to do for you?" He said, "Lord, let me see again." Jesus said to him, "Receive your sight; your faith has saved you." Immediately he regained his sight and followed him, glorifying God; and all the people, when they saw it, praised God.

To ponder

When we were given the capacity to love, to speak, to decide, to dream, to hope and create and suffer, we were also given the longing to be known by the One who most wants to be completely known.—Robert Benson, *Between the Dreaming and the Coming True*

Walk with God

During Lent one year I gave up listening to music and podcasts when I walked. I wanted to use the time for prayer or silence, to connect with God. Even without music or words, however, I found that my mind was constantly in motion, thinking about what I needed to do next, who I needed to call, or what work needed to get done. Too often I got so caught up in my thoughts that I missed seeing the beauty and the people in front of me.

"Lord, let me see again." The words of the man who was blind could be my words too. Help me see, Lord. Open my eyes. Open my heart to the gifts before me.

During this Lenten season, what's keeping you from seeing Jesus? Is it your phone? Work and school schedule? Envy of others? Pride? This Lent, take a walk or pause for a few moments. Listen for God's voice calling you: *Receive your sight.*

Prayer

Ever-present God, walk with us and open our eyes to the gift of your presence. Amen.

Luke 19:1-7

[Jesus] entered Jericho and was passing through it. A man was there named Zacchaeus; he was a chief tax collector and was rich. He was trying to see who Jesus was, but on account of the crowd he could not, because he was short in stature. So he ran ahead and climbed a sycamore tree to see him, because he was going to pass that way. When Jesus came to the place, he looked up and said to him, "Zacchaeus, hurry and come down; for I must stay at your house today." So he hurried down and was happy to welcome him. All who saw it began to grumble and said, "He has gone to be the guest of one who is a sinner."

To ponder

But how do I lead them to peace? By listening to their stories, telling them yours, and reminding them that you are all on this journey together.—Cleo Wade, *What the Road Said*

On the lookout

We live in a small town where we can walk to most places. When the weather is nice, we walk our daughter to kindergarten. As we walk, my daughter exudes happiness. Friends and neighbors comment on her smile. Many days she skips and swings her arms in joy, or runs ahead of us.

Zacchaeus ran ahead of everyone and climbed a tree. He didn't let anything keep him from seeing Jesus—not his height, not his despised position as a tax collector for Rome, not the other people crowded around Jesus. Then he got more than just a good look when Jesus came by, spotted him, and invited himself to Zacchaeus's house!

This is how God comes to us, wherever we are, whoever we are, and whatever we have done. Over and over again Jesus looks for us and invites us into a closer relationship with him.

Prayer

Thank you, God, for your boundless grace that looks for us and finds us wherever we are. Amen.

April 4

Luke 19:8-10

Zacchaeus stood there and said to the Lord, "Look, half of my possessions, Lord, I will give to the poor; and if I have defrauded anyone of anything, I will pay back four times as much." Then Jesus said to him, "Today salvation has come to this house, because he too is a son of Abraham. For the Son of Man came to seek out and to save the lost."

To ponder

Walk, even when you don't know where to step next. Just keep walking and you'll see what I saw: the valley is full. When I think I am on a solo quest, I realize the valley is full of travelers.
—Hannah Brencher, *Come Matter Here*

Found in God

One summer I walked five hundred miles across northern Spain to reach Santiago de Compostela, where a grand cathedral houses the relics of St. James. One pilgrim I met shared with me, "We all have the same needs—to find a place to stay and to get food." It was a gift to walk with a community in which the needs and hopes of others became mine too. We were the body of Christ bound to one another.

God's love for us doesn't delight in who is the best or who has acquired the most or who is the most faithful. Rather, God delights in our desire to know God, as the story of Zacchaeus shows us. We are God's children, not because of anything we've done, but because of whose we are. God's love encourages us to cheer for others in their joy, and to sit with them in their sadness.

In God's reign there is room for everyone and enough for everyone. God's way is one of abundance and a shared sense that this world is better because we journey through it together as one body with many members.

Prayer

Help us to be found in you, God, and only in you. Amen.

Luke 19:28, 35-40

[Jesus] went on ahead, going up to Jerusalem. . . . Then they brought [a colt] to Jesus; and . . . they set Jesus on it. As he rode along, people kept spreading their cloaks on the road. As he was now approaching the path down from the Mount of Olives, the whole multitude of the disciples began to praise God joyfully with a loud voice for all the deeds of power that they had seen, saying, "Blessed is the king who comes in the name of the Lord! Peace in heaven, and glory in the highest heaven!" Some of the Pharisees in the crowd said to him, "Teacher, order your disciples to stop." He answered, "I tell you, if these were silent, the stones would shout out."

To ponder

All creatures, worship God most high! / Sound ev'ry voice in earth and sky.—"All creatures, worship God most high!," ELW 835

Join the marching band

My children love to play marching band. They grab books, toys, and anything else they can use to make music and stomp up and down our hallways cheering, clapping, and singing.

Is this what it was like for people as Jesus entered Jerusalem? They spread their cloaks on the ground, the customary way of welcoming an important person, but Jesus was riding on a lowly colt. While many were shouting and praising God, some Pharisees were grumbling. Reading a bit further in Luke's gospel, we find that Jesus weeps when he sees the city in the distance, clears the temple of merchants, and has his authority questioned by religious leaders.

Despite any questions, fears, and misgivings people may have had on this day, they cheered and sang for joy because of Jesus' presence in their lives. Jesus is with us too, amid our questions, doubts, fears, regrets, grief, anger, and joy. Because of this, we can join the rocks and hills and all creation in praising God with fanfare.

Prayer

Thank you, God, for sending Jesus to walk this earth. Amen.

April 6

Luke 22:14, 19-20

When the hour came, [Jesus] took his place at the table, and the apostles with him. . . . Then he took a loaf of bread, and when he had given thanks, he broke it and gave it to them, saying, "This is my body, which is given for you. Do this in remembrance of me." And he did the same with the cup after supper, saying, "This cup that is poured out for you is the new covenant in my blood."

To ponder

Whenever you break bread and drink wine like this, remember me and remember that someday God's dream—of everyone sharing and caring, loving and laughing—will come true.—Desmond Tutu, *Children of God Storybook Bible*

74

Fed and sent

At the church where I worship there's a stained-glass window that depicts the last supper. It's not in the sanctuary where one might expect, but in the gym. The window looks out over community basketball games, health clinics, church potlucks, Bible studies, meetings, and much more. When people walk into the gym, they are greeted by Jesus and the disciples at the table.

The presence of this window in such a communal place reminds me that the gifts of communion are gifts to be experienced and shared with other people. In the breaking of bread, the body of Christ strengthens and nourishes us in faith and in love for God and one another. In the offering of wine, the blood of Christ is poured out in boundless grace for the whole world.

Jesus invites all people everywhere to his table, to be fed and then sent to feed others.

Prayer

Bread of life, you feed us with mercy and compassion. Send us out to share your life-giving bread with others. Amen.

Luke 22:39, 47-54

[Jesus] went, as was his custom, to the Mount of Olives; and the disciples followed him. . . . A crowd came, and the one called Judas, one of the twelve, was leading them. He approached Jesus to kiss him; but Jesus said to him, "Judas, is it with a kiss that you are betraying the Son of Man?" When those who were around him saw what was coming, they asked, "Lord, should we strike with the sword?" Then one of them struck the slave of the high priest and cut off his right ear. But Jesus said, "No more of this!" And he touched his ear and healed him. Then Jesus said to the chief priests, the officers of the temple police, and the elders who had come for him, "Have you come out with swords and clubs as if I were a bandit? When I was with you day after day in the temple, you did not lay hands on me. But this is your hour, and the power of darkness!"

Then they seized him and led him away, bringing him into the high priest's house.

To ponder

Let yourself be found / by the One / waiting for you / to come / into the silence, / emptiness, / darkness of God.—Steve Garnass-Holmes, "Deserted Place"

In the shadow of the cross

Taking a good, hard look directly at the cross of Jesus is difficult for us. What comes to your mind when you see an image of a cross? Do you think about Jesus and his life, his teachings, his miracles? Do you think about his arrest, trials, and death? Do you wonder why all this happened?

In today's text we are at the Mount of Olives with the crowd gathered around Jesus, a crowd that witnesses Judas betraying Jesus and someone wielding a sword. Finally Jesus is arrested and taken away.

This is an uncomfortable place to be, but we are not alone. Jesus is still with us.

Prayer

Wherever the cross takes us, Lord, we know you've gone before us and will not abandon us. Amen.

April 8

Luke 22:56-62

A servant-girl, seeing [Peter] in the firelight, stared at him and said, "This man also was with him." But he denied it, saying, "Woman, I do not know him." A little later someone else, on seeing him, said, "You also are one of them." But Peter said, "Man, I am not!" Then about an hour later still another kept insisting, "Surely this man also was with him; for he is a Galilean." But Peter said, "Man, I do not know what you are talking about!" At that moment, while he was still speaking, the cock crowed. The Lord turned and looked at Peter. Then Peter remembered the word of the Lord, how he had said to him, "Before the cock crows today, you will deny me three times." And he went out and wept bitterly.

To ponder

Rise, shine, you people! / Christ the Lord has entered / our human story; God in him is centered. / He comes to us, by death and sin surrounded, / with grace unbounded.—"Rise, shine, you people!," ELW 665

Waiting for the sun

One morning at 4:00 a.m. I heard my son talking to himself. "I'm not tired," he told me over breakfast that morning. I asked him why he was awake so early and he answered, "The sun was taking so long to come up."

Perhaps you know this feeling—the feeling of waiting, longing, hoping. Maybe Peter felt this way as he sat in the firelight. After all, Jesus had been taken away by the authorities. Then Peter denied even knowing him—not just once, but three times. How could Jesus ever forgive him after this?

Peter would go on to be a key figure in the early church, spreading the good news about Jesus to wider and wider circles of people. The power of God's forgiveness and grace shines through his story.

Whatever you have done, whatever you are feeling, God's love for you has no limits.

Prayer

God, sit with us in our times of waiting, longing—and despair too. Fill us with hope to face a new day with you. Amen.

April 9

Luke 22:66; 23:1, 3-4, 7

When day came, the assembly of the elders of the people, both chief priests and scribes, gathered together, and they brought him to their council. . . . Then the assembly rose as a body and brought Jesus before Pilate. . . . Pilate asked him, "Are you the king of the Jews?" He answered, "You say so." Then Pilate said to the chief priests and the crowds, "I find no basis for an accusation against this man." . . . And when he learned that he was under Herod's jurisdiction, he sent him off to Herod, who was himself in Jerusalem at that time.

To ponder

The best lack all conviction, while the worst / Are full of passionate intensity. —William Butler Yeats, "The Second Coming"

80

Excruciating decisions

Many of my parishioners in Washington, DC, had governmental jobs. They honored their callings, working long hours and seeking the best for our nation. They were forced to make countless agonizing decisions—with which some citizens inevitably disagreed.

Pilate was faced with an agonizing decision: What should he do with Jesus? Strong opinions about Jesus' guilt or innocence arose from every corner. Rather than declaring his own conviction that Jesus had done nothing wrong, Pilate opted for the coward's path. He listened to the crowd's demands and passed off Jesus to Herod.

We often fret, cower, vacillate, or pass the buck when faced with tough choices. Each option seems flawed, yet not to act is sometimes the worst choice of all. When we must make a difficult decision, what if we ask God to lead us and guide us, and then take a daring leap of faith?

Prayer

O God our help in ages past and our hope for years to come, when challenges appear insurmountable, fill us with your wisdom that we might act justly, truthfully, and kindly. Amen.

April 10 / Sunday of the Passion

Luke 23:8-11

When Herod saw Jesus, he was very glad, for he had been wanting to see him for a long time, because he had heard about him and was hoping to see him perform some sign. He questioned him at some length, but Jesus gave him no answer. The chief priests and the scribes stood by, vehemently accusing him. Even Herod with his soldiers treated him with contempt and mocked him; then he put an elegant robe on him, and sent him back to Pilate.

To ponder

They crucified my Lord, / and he never said a mumbalin' word; / they crucified my Lord, / and he never said a mumbalin' word; /

not a word, not a word, not a word.—"They crucified my Lord,"
ELW 350

So few words to speak

Suppose you are responsible for choosing readers for today's Passion story. Choose wisely! Those you ask to recite only one or two lines might feel slighted, readers for the parts of Judas or Pilate might be offended, and, of course, you must select the finest reader of all for Jesus' role. But after carefully making these selections, you may be shocked by how few words Jesus uttered during his final hours. We watch Jesus more but hear him less.

Words fail us sometimes—when friends lose a child, when a neighbor is treated unfairly, when a global pandemic takes millions of lives. We try to offer comforting words when misery and rage strike, but more often than not we end up tongue-tied.

Jesus' silence is instructive when words fail us. Are there times when silence is the best course of action? Take a few minutes now to be silent in God's presence.

Prayer

Dear Lord Jesus Christ, draw us into the mystery of your deep silence. Inspire us to keep silent, to listen, and to watch as we patiently wait for God. Amen.

Luke 23:13-21, 24

Pilate then called together the chief priests, the leaders, and the people, and said to them, "You brought me this man as one who was perverting the people; and here I have examined him in your presence and have not found this man guilty of any of your charges against him. Neither has Herod, for he sent him back to us. Indeed, he has done nothing to deserve death. I will therefore have him flogged and release him." Then they all shouted out together, "Away with this fellow! Release Barabbas for us!" (This was a man who had been put in prison for an insurrection that had taken place in the city, and for murder.) Pilate, wanting to release Jesus, addressed them again; but they kept shouting, "Crucify, crucify him!" . . . So Pilate gave his verdict that their demand should be granted.

To ponder

Lamb of God most holy, upon the cross extended, / all my sin you carry, the burden of my soul. / What love amazing! What price unbounded! / Your body, wounded, will make me whole.
—"Lamb of God most holy," ACS 932

Those nails

Who was responsible for Jesus' death: the religious authorities, the political leaders, the boisterous crowds, the macho soldiers?

In a congregation I once served, near the end of our Palm/Passion Sunday services we would noisily drop a large wooden cross in front of the altar. Then we went forward one by one, knelt, and nailed a piece of paper to the cross. On those papers we had written those sins that weighed us down. As we returned to our seats, shaken and tearful, we bowed our heads.

The echoes of those banging nails lingered with us throughout Holy Week, as they likely will with you. But because of this, may you cherish all the more Jesus' wondrous love in carrying the sins and burdens of sinners such as you and me.

Prayer

Dear Jesus Christ, let us cherish your wondrous love and share it with others who feel weighed down. Amen.

April 12

Luke 23:26-27, 32-34

As they led [Jesus] away, they seized a man, Simon of Cyrene, who was coming from the country, and they laid the cross on him, and made him carry it behind Jesus. A great number of the people followed him, and among them were women who were beating their breasts and wailing for him. . . . Two others also, who were criminals, were led away to be put to death with him. When they came to the place that is called The Skull, they crucified Jesus there with the criminals, one on his right and one on his left. Then Jesus said, "Father, forgive them; for they do not know what they are doing."

To ponder

God responds to our limitation, failing, and sin not with judgment but with mercy, with compassion, with forgiveness. . . . Jesus now offers forgiveness just as [he] has done throughout his ministry. Because that's not just what Jesus does, it's what God is: mercy, compassion, love . . . in a word, forgiveness.—David J. Lose, "In the Meantime: Luke 23:34a"

God is forgiveness

Roman soldiers, crowds "gathered there for this spectacle" (Luke 23:48), and followers of Jesus were all eyewitnesses to the crucifixion.

Jesus easily could have lashed out at those who mocked him and those who put him to death. Instead his words were filled with love and compassion: "Father, forgive them; for they do not know what they have done."

These words should give us pause because, despite our betrayals, lies, and cowardice, Jesus' words are for us too: "Father, forgive them."

Prayer

O Lord Jesus Christ, in your final breaths, you pled with God to forgive us all. Help us to treasure the gift of your mercy and to share this gift with your groaning world. Amen.

April 13

Luke 23:34-38

And they cast lots to divide [Jesus'] clothing. And the people stood by, watching; but the leaders scoffed at him, saying, "He saved others; let him save himself if he is the Messiah of God, his chosen one!" The soldiers also mocked him, coming up and offering him sour wine, and saying, "If you are the King of the Jews, save yourself!" There was also an inscription over him, "This is the King of the Jews."

To ponder

Christ was powerless on the cross; and yet there he performed his mightiest work and conquered sin, death, world, hell, devil, and all evil.—Martin Luther, "The Magnificat"

Hands outstretched

We live in such a frenzied world. Our worth is often measured by how busy we are. Even when we retire, we feel obliged to say, "I have never been busier." Are we worthless when we are retired or unemployed, when we are sick or dying, when we can do nothing?

With hands outstretched and nailed to the cross, Jesus appeared helpless as he faced spineless government leaders and judgmental religious authorities, harsh military functionaries, and jeering bystanders. And yet Martin Luther believed that God is most fully revealed in ways we would least expect—especially in Jesus' death on the cross.

God was at work during the crucifixion. Jesus' weakest, most vulnerable state shows us God and the depth of God's love for us and the world. God is at work too when we can do nothing more or less than rest in the arms of Jesus.

Prayer

O God, open our eyes to see you at work amid weakness, help-lessness, and vulnerability. Open our hearts to take in what you reveal to us on the cross. Amen.

April 14 / Maundy Thursday

Luke 23:39-43

One of the criminals who were hanged there kept deriding [Jesus] and saying, "Are you not the Messiah? Save yourself and us!" But the other rebuked him, saying, "Do you not fear God, since you are under the same sentence of condemnation? And we indeed have been condemned justly . . . but this man has done nothing wrong." Then he said, "Jesus, remember me when you come into your kingdom." He replied, "Truly I tell you, today you will be with me in Paradise."

To ponder

In marriage you say the same things over and over, you inquire about the same people; and this is ho-hum in one way. But it is breathtaking in another.—Joseph Sittler, *Grace Notes and Other Fragments*

A few exquisite words

In just one day we hear and read countless words through conversations, social media, news reports, books, music, video, and on and on. Of course, not all words have the same effect on us. Sometimes a few exquisite words have more impact than all the rest. Lovers often speak just a word or two or none at all. Simply sitting together hand-in-hand in front of the fireplace is enough; in fact, it is dazzling.

On this Maundy Thursday, Jesus gathers with us at supper and showers affection upon us with a few simple words: "Eat . . . drink . . . for the remembrance of me."

Place just a few more of Jesus' words on your heart today. Like a teenager hearing "I love you" for the first time, be smitten as Jesus whispers to you, "Today you will be with me in Paradise."

Prayer

O wondrous God, you choose simple gifts of word and water, bread and wine, to reveal your love. Teach us to cherish these treasures offered to us through your Word, Jesus Christ our Lord. Amen.

April 15 / Good Friday

Luke 23:44-49

It was now about noon, and darkness came over the whole land until three in the afternoon, while the sun's light failed; and the curtain of the temple was torn in two. Then Jesus, crying with a loud voice, said, "Father, into your hands I commend my spirit." Having said this, he breathed his last. When the centurion saw what had taken place, he praised God and said, "Certainly this man was innocent." And when all the crowds who had gathered there for this spectacle saw what had taken place, they returned home, beating their breasts. But all his acquaintances, including the women who had followed him from Galilee, stood at a distance, watching these things.

To ponder

Only those having sustained the terrors of the cross can understand the raucous laughter of resurrection.—Belden C. Lane, *The Solace of Fierce Landscapes*

The crucified Savior

I always dreamed of a full sanctuary on Good Friday, but that never occurred during my forty-two years of active ministry. Each year when I entered Good Friday services, my heart sank as I looked out over a smattering of souls gathered to stand in awe of the Savior who gave his life for the salvation of the whole world.

In the church year Good Friday is a day to stand vigil before the cross. Though it is tempting to skip the cross and go directly to Easter joy, the church urges us to stop and keep watch as the centurion, the crowds, and Jesus' followers did at the crucifixion.

"Father, into your hands I commend my spirit." Jesus entrusts himself to the arms of God with his very last breath. When we breathe our last, we can entrust ourselves to God's arms just as Jesus did.

Prayer

O Lamb of God, who takes away the sin of the world, draw us very near your cross today, that we may discover hope even in the face of death. We ask this in your holy name. Amen.

April 16 / Resurrection of Our Lord

Luke 24:1-5

On the first day of the week, at early dawn, [the women] came to the tomb, taking the spices that they had prepared. They found the stone rolled away from the tomb, but when they went in, they did not find the body. . . . Suddenly two men in dazzling clothes stood beside them. The women were terrified and bowed their faces to the ground, but the men said to them, "Why do you look for the living among the dead? He is not here, but has risen."

To ponder

Let us not seek to make [Easter] less monstrous, / for our own convenience, our own sense of beauty, / lest, awakened in one unthinkable hour, we are / embarrassed by the miracle.—John Updike, "Seven Stanzas at Easter"

This is God's doing

The empty tomb was a frightening and befuddling place for those faithful and heartbroken women who came to anoint Jesus' body that first Easter morning. Like them, we may have nagging questions about what really happened to his body. Our Easter celebration, however, has nothing to do with how much we comprehend about how God raised Jesus from the dead.

Quite simply, resurrection is God's doing, not ours. Sin, death, and evil do not have the final word. What miraculous news of God's boundless grace for us and the world!

Father Aidan Kavanagh, my seminary worship professor, advised future pastors to celebrate Easter by "pulling out the stops and letting it rip!" (Pulling out a "stop" on a pipe organ opens the flow of air to a particular set of pipes.) This is indeed the day to pull out all the stops and let it rip and shout at the top of our lungs so all the world can hear, "Alleluia! Christ is risen! Alleluia!"

Prayer

O wondrous God, who raised your beloved Son from hell's grasp, fill us with joy on this festival day, that we might tell all the world that Christ is risen from the dead. Amen.

Notes

Welcome: Charles Wesley, 1707–1788, "Love divine, all loves excelling," ELW 631, st. 1. **March 2:** Martin Luther, 95 *Theses*, theses 1 and 3, writer's translation of the Latin, www.luther.de/en/95th-lat.html. **March 3:** Henri J. M. Nouwen, *Life of the Beloved* (New York: Crossroad, 2002), 31–33. **March 4:** Henri J. M. Nouwen, *In the Name of Jesus* (New York: Crossroad, 1989), 27–28. **March 5:** Tish Harrison Warren, *Liturgy of the Ordinary* (Downers Grove, IL: InterVarsity, 2016), 34. **March 6:** James Cone, *The Cross and the Lynching Tree* (Maryknoll, NY: Orbis, 2011), 149–150. Article referenced in reflection: John Burnett, "Statue of a Homeless Jesus Startles a Wealthy Community," NPR, April 13, 2014, www.npr.org/2014/04/13/302019921/statue -of-a-homeless-jesus-startles-a-wealthy-community. This bronze statue by Timothy Schmalz has been installed in many locations around the world. **March 7:** Oswald Allen, 1816–1878, alt., "Today your mercy calls us," LBW 304, st. 2. **March 8:** Rachel Held Evans, *Inspired* (Santa Rosa, CA: Thomas Nelson, 2018), 41. **March 9:** Desmond Tutu, *God Has a Dream* (Minneola, NY: Ixia, 2017), 78. **March 10:** Henri J. M. Nouwen, Donald P. McNeill, and Douglas A. Morrison, *Compassion* (New York: Doubleday, 1982), 3–4. **March 11:** Philip Yancey, *Where Is God When It Hurts?* (Grand Rapids, MI: Zondervan, 1990), 248. **March 12:** Rachel Held Evans, *Inspired*, 221. **March 14:** Audre Lorde, *Burst of Light* (Mineola, NY: Ixia, 2017), 78. **March 15:** David Scherer, *AGAP-OLOGY: Little Things I've Learned about God's Big Love* (New York: National Council of Churches, 2015), 74. **March 16:** Rozella Haydée White (@lovebigcoach), "I believe that love is the answer to EVERYTHING," Twitter, June 3, 2020. **March 17:** Martin Luther King Jr., *Strength to Love* (Minneapolis: Fortress, 2010). **March 18:** Eric H. F. Law, *Holy Currencies: Six Blessings for Sustainable Missional Ministries* (St. Louis, MO: Chalice, 2013), 7. **March 20:** Tom Marshall, dir., *Ted Lasso*, season 1, episode 3, "Trent Crimm: The Independent," aired August 14, 2020, on Apple TV+. **March 21:** A. Rochaun Meadows-Fernandez, "The Unbearable Grief of Black Mothers," May 28, 2020, www.vox.com/first-person/2020/5/28 /21272380/black-mothers-grief-sadness-covid-19. **March 22:** Greg Boyle, *Tattoos on the Heart* (New York: Free Press, 2010), 88. **March 23:** Martin Luther, "Third Sunday after Trinity: Luke 15:1-10," *The Complete Sermons of Martin Luther*, reprint ed. (Ada, MI: Baker, 2000). **March 24:** Desmond Tutu, *Hope and Suffering* (Grand Rapids, MI: Eerdmans, 1984). **March 25:** Nadia Bolz-Weber, *Shameless* (New York: Convergent, 2019), 177. **March 26:** Parker J. Palmer, *The Company of Strangers* (New York: Crossroad, 1986), 20–24. **March 27:** Mary Oliver, "Walking Home from Oak-Head," *Thirst* (Boston: Beacon, 2006), 2. **March 28:** bell hooks, *Sisters of the Yam* (Boston: South End, 1993), 167. **March 29:** John Eldredge, *Wild at Heart* (Nashville: Thomas Nelson, 2001), 71. **March 30:** Mark I. Rosen, *Thank You for Being Such a Pain* (New York: Three Rivers, 1998), 254–255. **March 31:** Ram Dass, "Stroked," *Parabola* 45, no. 1 (Spring 2021), 17. **April 1:** Mary Peterman, *Healing* (Philadelphia: Fortress, 1974), 51–56. **April 2:** Robert Benson, *Between the Dreaming and the Coming True* (New York: Jeremy P. Tarcher/Putnam, 1996), 35. **April 3:** Cleo Wade, *What the Road Said* (New York: Feiwel and Friends, 2021). **April 4:** Hannah Brencher, *Come Matter Here* (Grand Rapids, MI: Zondervan, 2018), 68. **April 5:** Francis of Assisi, 1182–1226; tr. composite, © 1997 Augsburg Fortress, "All creatures, worship God most high!," ELW 835, st. 1. **April 6:** Desmond Tutu, *Children of God Storybook Bible* (Grand Rapids, MI: Zonderkidz, 2010), 109. **April 7:** Steve Garnass-Holmes, "Deserted Place," February 4, 2021, unfoldinglight .net. **April 8:** Ronald A. Klug, b. 1939, alt., © 1974 Augsburg Publishing House, "Rise, shine, you people!," ELW 665, st. 1. **April 9:** William Butler Yeats, "The Second Coming," *The Collected Works of W. B. Yeats, Vol. 1: The Poems* (New York: Scribner, 1997), 189. **April 10:** African American spiritual, "They crucified my Lord," ELW 350, st. 1. **April 11:** Anonymous; tr. Martin A. Seltz, b. 1951; English text © 2009 Augsburg Fortress, "Lamb of God most holy," ACS 932, st. 1. **April 12:** David J. Lose, "In the Meantime: Luke 23:34a," March 18, 2013, www.davidlose.net/2013/03/luke-23-34a/. **April 13:** Martin Luther, "The Magnificat," trans. Beth Kreitzer, ed. Mary Jane Haemig, *The Annotated Luther, Volume 4: Pastoral Writings* (Minneapolis: Fortress, 2016), 363. **April 14:** Joseph Sittler, *Grace Notes and Other Fragments* (Philadelphia: Fortress, 1981), 19. **April 15:** Belden C. Lane, *The Solace of Fierce Landscapes*, reprint ed. (New York: Oxford, 1998), 171. **April 16:** John Updike, "Seven Stanzas at Easter," *Telephone Poles and Other Poems* (New York: Alfred A. Knopf, 1963), 72–73.